Starting Out Right

A Concise Guide to Starting Your Own Business

Catherine M. Martin

ISBN:1541088549
ISBN-13:9781541088542

DEDICATION

This book is dedicated to my mother. She always stands faithfully by me no matter what decisions I make.

CONTENTS

Introduction

Regardless of the industry, product, or service, running a business is a complex endeavor. Very few businesses last more than three years. Though failure rates vary by industry, the general consensus is that nine out of ten will fail – with poor management as the primary reason. Owning a business is a continuous learning curve. The business owner must be prepared to handle change and new and exciting developments when they occur.

Entrepreneurs and small business owners are at a disadvantage. They don't usually have the resources or skills to handle the day to day business operations, let alone the more difficult management decisions. They have to wear too many hats and juggle too many responsibilities that they are not qualified to handle.

The goal of this book is to help you get started on your journey armed and ready to achieve your goals. Also, to enrich you with the knowledge and skills to get your business started on the right track, to help eliminate problems down the road, and to aid you in making sound *management* decisions as your business grows. Decisions made now have a huge impact down the road.

The information you uncover as you answer the questions and follow the guidelines can be used to prepare a solid, useful business plan. A business plan is a must if you are seeking outside financing and extremely useful in guiding your day-to-day activities. Research has shown that having a business plan can improve your business performance. Companies that have a plan tend to grow about 30% faster than those that don't have a plan. Plenty of businesses succeed without a plan, but, businesses with a plan grow faster and are more successful.

Planning can also keep you focused. Review your plan and goals often to make sure the decisions you are making are moving you closer to your goals.

Planning aids in keeping things simple. The simpler you can make things the more likely they are to get done. A lot of business owners who are not use to the "business" side of a company have a tendency to complicate operations.

Having a plan is not the only answer. You have to use the plan. Your plan is your roadmap to success. You need to update it periodically as things change. Your customers will be a huge source of information for formulating and establishing goals and strategies.

Starting a new business can be a scary process. There is an abundance of risk and unknowns involved. Be sure to take some uninterrupted time just to think. Mull over your ideas and thoughts. Reflect on how your goals and dreams interact with your life. Take the time to record your ideas and thoughts as you progress through this book. It will help lessen and eliminate some of your fears and questions. It will give you a workable plan as you start your journey.

That's why it is important to write down the answers the questions in this book. I keep a three ring binder so that I can three hole punch information from any source. So, grab pen and paper and let's get started on the wildest adventure of your life!

CHAPTER 1
BEING DESCRIPTIVE

Before anything else you need to decide exactly what it is that you are going to do. By answering the following questions, you will get a feel for what you are trying to accomplish. By writing these answers down you can go back to them to keep you focused and motivated.

1.   Who are your customers?

You can't be all things to all people. It is very important to narrow your idea of your potential customers. Identify the demographic characteristics of consumers who will benefit from your product or services. You need to fully describe your potential customers. Write down as much information about your customers as you can.

The state of the economy, interest rates and technology can influence your potential customers, but, social and cultural norms are the most important marketing environment. These include such things as gender, age, life stage, income, and trends.

Define your customers using the following as a guide:

- Demographics – age, gender, income
- Psychographics – their personality type, preferences
- Behavior – their likes and dislikes, hobbies

One way to help visualize your ideal customer is to look at yourself as the consumer. Are your products or services something you would want or need? If so, describe yourself.

If you are a business to business (B2B) company, you also need to describe your customer in detail – industry, size, location. You would want to include:

- Number of employees
- Revenue
- Geographic scope

Look for the places your ideal customer hangs out, either physical location or online. By clearly defining this ideal customer you can better build your marketing strategy, products, services and location. You won't waste time and money going after the wrong customers.

2.   What product or service are you providing?

You have to know what you do and who you are if you are going to set your business apart from your competition. Fully describe your product or service. Describe how your product or service fulfills a need or solves a problem for the customers you described above.

- How will you make a difference in their lives?

- Describe how your product or service is different than your competitors.

- What makes you unique?

- Clearly define the needs and benefits that would make your customers purchase from you.

- Ensure that your product or service has clear value for your customers. What value do you add?

- What are you doing for your customers?

3.   How will you deliver this product or service? What is your distribution strategy?

If you need a physical store, decide where you are going to be located and why you need this location. Describe how your customers will pay you. Will you offer terms? If so, write up your credit policies. Will you accept credit cards? Investigate the different merchant services – there are many with many different prices.

If you are selling a product online, investigate the different shipping options – USPS, UPS, Fedex. What about suppliers for boxes, stuffing, envelopes, etc?

4. Competition

You need to know your competition as well as you know your customers.

- What do you offer that they don't?

- Why would people come to you instead of them?

- What kind of comments are they getting on social media about their service or products?

Buy or order from your competition and see if they have good quality, good customer service, and an easy ordering system.

5. Why are you going into business? What do you hope to accomplish?

This is probably the most important question to answer before you start your own business. By answering this question you can better understand what motivates you. It is the first step in deciding your company's mission, vision, and purpose. Knowing the goals and aspirations for your business will aid you in making many decisions now and down the road.

Clarifying your *why* communicates who you are and what you stand for. The *why* drives everything you do in designing your products and services. Your *why* dictates your company's actions and drives you and your team.

Don't try to be all things to all people. Have a clearly defined customer and product or service. If not, it makes it very hard to focus and deliver what makes you unique.

By having this information readily available when you need to make decisions, you can easily see how different options would affect your basic idea of what your business is. You can see if a decision will affect what you hope to provide to your customers.

Keep in mind that as you and your company change and grow, you can come back to this and make changes to fit your current situation. You may find that once you get started; your customers will direct you to a whole different line of products or services that they need from you.

CHAPTER 2
YOUR EXIT STRATEGY

I know that a lot of you are saying, "I haven't even started and you want me to plan the end!" But, as you go through the process of starting your business, the decision on how you will exit your business will come into play in making decisions. Your exit strategy needs to be clear because it will dictate how you operate your business. Your exit strategy has implications on your business structure, your assets, and your employees.

What is an exit strategy? An exit strategy is a plan to walk away from the business with what you want to walk away with. In many cases, business owners want to walk away with the financial means to retire or start another business venture. You may have other goals you want to achieve before walking away. What are they?

There are various ways to exit a business. How you decide to exit your business plays a huge part in the process of starting your business; and, everything to do with how your business operates.

1 –A lifestyle business generates income until you are financially, physically and mentally ready to retire and then you just quit. If this is your goal you wouldn't want to purchase a lot of equipment or assets that you would be stuck with when you decide to retire. You would want to keep debt low. You will want to minimize your dependence on other investors and structure the business to draw out cash as needed.

2 – You may be planning to build your business to a certain point or a certain time and then you want to sell it. You will need to focus on building a business that someone would want to buy. You need to build value and equity every step of the way. You would want to make sure you have very accurate financial records with a clear distinction between business property and personal property.

To build a business that will someday be saleable you need to consider and plan for several factors:

  - **Profitability** – Is your business profitable? Is there room for growth in your industry?

  - **Competitive Advantage** – Build your business with a concentration on standing out from the competition through service, reputation, price, etc.

- **Systems and Structure** – Can your business operate without you? Do you have systems and procedures in place to insure the flow of operations? (See Chapter 7)

- **Debt** – No one wants to buy a business loaded down with huge debt.

- Pay attention to any **inefficiency** you may have.

Several years ago, I was hired by a small business owner who had been approached by a large corporation interested in purchasing her business. My job was to get the financial records in order so that a fair price could be reached. In doing so, it was found that several assets were recorded as expenses for tax purposes at the time of purchase. In doing so, they could not be included on the asset and inventory valuations. They were basically given to the new owners for free. Had she built her business with the intentions of selling down the road, she would have made sure to list every asset and taken other avenues for reducing her tax burden.

This business owner had also purchased the land and building for her business in her personal name and the company rented it from her. When the new company purchased her business they did not purchase the land or building. When their lease was up, they moved. The owner was then stuck with a huge piece of commercial property with no tenants. She had to continue paying insurance and property taxes on the empty property for well over five years before someone else took it.

All of this could of been avoided if the owner had built a plan with an exit strategy clearly defined.

3 – You may have children that you envision taking over your business when you retire. There would need to be a very clear, precise plan for this take over that you could develop over time. For now, all you need to realize is that this is your plan.

4 – You may wish to grow your business to the point that one day you will have a public offering of stock to finance even more growth. The regulations and paperwork required for this means that you will have to have especially good accounting and business systems and records. This is also an expensive process, so, you will want to make plans to have the necessary funds when the time comes.

These are just a few of the different exit strategies available to you, the business owner. As you go through the process of starting your business this exit strategy will come into play when making decisions.

The best exit strategy is the one that best fits your small business and personal goals. The first step in creating your exit strategy is to determine your own personal long term goals and financial needs. How you define "success" comes into play here. You would then look at ways to achieve these goals, both in the short term and the long term.

Planning your exit strategy is about making a proactive series of decisions instead of reacting to unexpected events. Planning your exit strategy in advance gives you time to do it right and maximize your returns.

Everything, from which form of business structure you choose, to the name of your business, the accounting system you use, can be based on this exit strategy. But, keep in mind that as you and your business grow, your exit strategy and definition of success can change. Having your long range plan in mind from the beginning and as you progress can save headaches and work down the road.

SIDE NOTE

Another strategy to keep in mind when planning your business startup is what I refer to as "worst case scenario" strategies. These strategies or plans are for when an unforeseen event occurs, your business can continue. Some of the worst case scenario strategies would include: illness, accident, divorce, death, fire, or natural disaster.

Keep the worst case scenario events in mind as you make decisions affecting your business. Address these issues especially if you have partners or shareholders who share in the ownership of your business. Have strategies and plans in place in case of unforeseen events.

CHAPTER 3
NAMING YOUR BUSINESS

One of the most important marketing tools for small business owners is the naming of their business. It is the first thing potential customers will learn about you. The right name can make your company the talk of the town. The wrong one can doom it to obscurity and failure.

Ideally, your name should convey the expertise, value, and uniqueness of your products or services, as well as the emotional meaning you are trying to convey. Take the time to carefully think through this process and you will be able to create a name that works both for the short and the long term.

Start by deciding what you want your name to communicate. What kind of image do you want your business to project? It should reinforce the key elements of your business. The more your name communicates to customers about your business, the less effort you must exert to explain it. Does your name give you a competitive advantage explaining exactly what your business is or does? When you are deciding on your business name, think in terms of giving yourself a marketing advantage. Go back to where you were describing your business in Chapter 1. Look at the "what" and "who".

When choosing your company name keep the following in mind:

- Customers prefer names that they can relate to and understand
- Choose a name that not only appeals to you, but, your customers as well
- Don't pick a name that is long or confusing
- Don't pick a name that is too "cute"
- Consider the core of what your business does
- You want a name that makes people feel good

Compile a list of at least 15 to 25 possible names or variations of names you would like to have associated with your business. Write down words that remind you of the image you are trying to project. Also, look at your exit strategy. You don't want to name your shop Susie's Fashions if your exit strategy is to sell your business in 5 years. The buyer might not be named Susie and it doesn't really tell what kind of fashions you are selling.

If you are having trouble thinking of 15-25 ideas, you can go to www.businessnamegenerator.com. Enter key words that are the major theme of your business. Literally thousands of possibilities will pop up.

I find it easiest to prepare a worksheet (I use Excel) divided into four columns.

Name	State	Web	Website

List the names or variations that you are interested in.

Next, go to the state agency's site that handles business registrations or corporations for your state. (See Chapter 6). They should have some way of searching their database to see if another business is using the name you have listed. I find it helpful to just type in a partial name. That way anything that is similar to what I'm looking for will also pop up. You will want to make sure that people don't confuse you with another company just because your names are similar.

After you have eliminated any choices that are not available; you will want to do some internet research to see if a company in another state is using the names you have left.

I wanted to use Martin Business Solutions as the name of my accounting/management services company. The name was available with the state, but, there was a company in Kansas with the same name. I didn't have any plans to do this type of work outside of North Carolina. The only problem I faced was that the company in Kansas was already using martinbusinesssolutions.com. I had to put a hyphen in my web address to be able to use my name for my website.

Had I planned on becoming a national corporation, with branches in numerous states; having a company in Kansas with the same name would have created numerous problems and confusion for my customers.

After you have done your internet research, you will want to check with a web service provider to see what options you have for a website name. You might also need to check Facebook, Pinterest, Twitter, etc to see what options you have if you are planning on using these services. You may want to add columns to your worksheet to cover them as well.

You will also need to check with the U.S. Patent and Trademark Office to make sure you are not infringing on someone's trademark. You can go to www.uspto.gov/trademarks-application-process/search-trademark-database to do a database search. You can also, for about $300, protect your business name with a trademark at www.uspto.gov/trademarks-application-process/filing-online. They have full instructions on the process.

When you have your list narrowed down, decide which best describes your business and fits your exit strategy and growth plans. Ask friends and family to make sure your choice conveys the image you want for your business.

CHAPTER 4
STRUCTURING YOUR BUSINESS

There are basically four types of business ownership :

- Sole Proprietor

- Partnership

- Limited Liability Company

- Corporation

The type of ownership you choose will depend on:

- Liability – vulnerability

- Taxation

- Nature of the business

- Exit strategy

A good rule of thumb is to think worst case scenario and how it would play out in terms of your personal and business finances.

1. Sole Proprietor

The simplest business structure is a sole proprietorship. You and the business are one and the same. It is the easiest form to organize and sustain. This simplicity and affordability are why many small businesses operate as a sole proprietor. This is an excellent choice if your exit strategy is to work until you're financially and physically ready to retire and just want to stop without a whole lot of paperwork.

There are of course exceptions if your business carries a high level of risk. If the odds of someone being able to get hurt or property being damaged beyond what a good insurance policy would pay, you could run the risk of losing personal property in the event of an accident. Also, if you intend to borrow a lot of money or bring in outside capital you run the risk of losing personal assets.

If you are planning to find outside financing, either through investors or by borrowing, a sole proprietorship will not work. Investors usually don't invest in sole proprietorships because there is no way to divide ownership. If you are borrowing money, it would have to be a personal loan, not a business loan.

If you plan are doing work with larger companies, they may insist that you form an LLC or corporation. The IRS may look at you as an employee instead of a contractor and require the company to pay payroll taxes on your earnings.

There are several advantages to operating as a sole proprietor:

- Easiest and least expensive form to organize
- You are in complete control
- Receive all income generated by the business to keep or reinvest
- Profits from the business flow directly to the owner's personal tax return
- Easy to dissolve the business

There are also several disadvantages to operating as a sole proprietor:

- Have unlimited liability and are legally responsible for all debts against the business. Both business and personal assets are at risk.
- Some employee benefits are not directly deductible from business income for tax purposes.
- Recordkeeping must be meticulous to keep personal expenses and assets separate from business income, expenses and assets.

Starting as a sole proprietor is very easy. Unless you are using a fictious name (a name other than your own) all you have to do is start working. If you have decided to use a fictious name for your business then you will need to register that name with the counties you intend to do business in.

For example, if you are a plumber and decide to be a sole proprietor and operate as Joe Smith; then, all you need to do is start. But, if on the other hand, you want to operate under the name of Smith's Plumbing Services. Then you will need to register the name with the county and/or state.

2. Partnership

A partnership is formed when two or more people start a business together. Partnerships are now giving way to LLC's, but, if you decide a partnership is right for you, you must take every step to protect you and your business. A partnership agreement drawn up by an attorney is a must from a liability stand point (although it is not a legal requirement). Be sure that the written agreement covers everything. Again, take the worst case scenario attitude when deciding what to include and cover in your agreement. Figure 4-1 provides a partial list of the items to consider and include in your partnership agreement.

There was a small heating and air company in our area started and owned by two men. Over the years the business did well enough to support two growing families. When the children were old enough, they also worked in the company. One of the partners suddenly died. With no partnership agreement the widow was left with absolutely nothing. The remaining partner fired the children and the family was given nothing for his years of hard work. Don't let something like this happen to you.

To start a partnership (or any business with other people), it would be a good idea to see an attorney. It is so important that you cover all of the scenarios that could happen. You really need an attorney to insure that no one is left holding the bag. Have an outline of your operating procedures and your worst case scenarios worked out before you go. Your partnership will basically operate as a separate entity, meaning, you will have to have a fictious name and federal and state id numbers.

3.   LLC and LLP

A limited liability company and a limited liability partnership are very similar.

A limited liability partnership is made up of general partners and limited partners. The general partners operate the business and are subject to full liability, while limited partners are generally not personally liable for the debts and obligations of the partnership.

A limited liability company is part partnership and part corporation. The company is generally made up of members and a manager. The manager runs the operation of the business and does not have to be a member. Members are usually limited to the personal liability for the company.

As its name implies, members have limited liability and generally applies to debt. It does not imply no liability. Generally, a member's liability is limited to their investment in the LLC. Such as, if you are a member and have invested $10,000 in the LLC and the manager borrows $20,000 and doesn't pay it back; you personally are only liable for $10,000 of that debt. But, with banking issues as they are today, it would be very unlikely that a bank or a major vendor is going to extend credit without a "personal guarantee" against the debt. In which case, the person giving the personal guarantee would be responsible for paying the debt. There is no business structure that guarantees absolute freedom of liability.

The federal government does not recognize an LLC as a classification for federal tax purposes. An LLC business entity must file a corporation, partnership or sole proprietorship tax return.

If you decide to form a LLC with other people, treat it as you would a partnership. Have an agreement drawn up that covers all of those worst case scenario items. Go into detail about compensation, debt, profit sharing, and each partners' role in the business. This agreement is called the "Operating Agreement". It defines the internal rules for the company, such as, who's responsible for what, how decisions will be made, how profits and losses will be split, and what happens if someone wants out. See Figure 4-1.

I had a client who had formed an LLC with another person. They had a rather loose agreement that didn't cover a lot of scenarios. As it turned out, one partner began making and implementing some bad business decisions. Then, when things were looking really bad, he wanted to buy out his partner. His bad decisions had devalued the company to the point that there was very little cash offered after years of hard work.

It was discovered that this was his plan all along. He had several very lucrative jobs in the works that he didn't want to share the proceeds with a partner. He drove the business down so that he could get it for practically nothing. Then have these future jobs waiting to bring it back up after he was sole owner.

A thorough, detailed agreement could have protected the other partner.

4. Corporations

A corporation is a legal entity all of its own. Its existence is separate and apart from its owners. By being a separate entity this limits the liabilities of the owners.

For income tax purposes there are two types of corporations:

A Sub Chapter S Corporation (or Sub S) filing of the tax return causes the profits or the loss to flow directly onto the tax returns of the owners in proportion to ownership.

S corporations are corporations that elect to pass corporate income, losses, deductions and credit through to their shareholders for federal tax purposes. Shareholders of S corporations report the flow-through of income and losses on their personal tax returns and are assessed tax at their individual income tax rates. This allows S corporations to avoid double taxation on the corporate income. S corporations are responsible for tax on certain built-in gains and passive income.

To qualify for S corporation status, the corporation must meet the following requirements:

- Be a domestic corporation. Meaning it is an United States corporation.
- Have only allowable shareholders including individuals, certain trust, and estates and may not include partnerships, corporations or non-resident alien shareholders
- Have no more than 100 shareholders
- Have one class of stock
- May not be an ineligible corporation i.e. certain financial institutions, insurance companies, and domestic international sales corporations.

In order to become an S corporation, the corporation must submit Form 2553 Election by a Small Business Corporation signed by all the shareholders. You will find this form at www.irs.gov.

If your exit strategy is to someday take your company public, you would not want to elect Sub S status. You would eventually have to change your status, and possibly form a new corporation, because the Sub S can only have 100 shareholders.

All states do not recognize Sub S corporations equally. Be sure to check with your Secretary of State and your Department of Revenue to see if choosing a Sub S Corporation is beneficial in your state.

A C Corporation is entirely a free standing entity. It files its own tax return, independent of its owners.

There are certain tax advantages to forming a C Corporation over an LLC or S Corporation. The level of protection, as far as liability goes, is also greater than a S Corporation or an LLC.

Also, a C Corporation does not have the same limitations of ownership that were mentioned under the Sub S Corporation.

Every state has its own rules about how to form an LLC or Corporation. They all recommend or require Corporate By-Laws or LLC Articles of Organization. Below are some websites where you can see examples and/or download templates.

Free template downloads for Corporate By-Laws:

www.inc.com/tools/corporate-bylaws-template.html

Free template for LLC Articles of Organization:

www.northwestregisteredagent.com/articles-of-organization.html

These are some good examples, but, you don't have to be this detailed. These are just the general rules your organization will operate by. If there is more than one of you organizing the company, you may need even more detail to insure against the worst case scenario events.

Be very precise in filling out your paperwork. Be sure to include every period, comma, etc. I had a client who had filed their paperwork with the state and federal government using periods between the letters in their name (A.B.C. Company). When they filed their first payroll reports, they were rejected because they had put ABC Company on the reports. The government agencies said that the name did not match the id numbers.

Be sure to review the information from the earlier chapters to aid in deciding which structure is best for you. Look at what types of liability you could face, ie, will you need debt to purchase equipment, etc. Are the odds of personal injury to an employee or customer high or low?

Which form best fits with your exit strategy and future plans?

For Example: If your exit strategy is to build a company to which you plan to sale at a later date, a corporation may be the way to go. This keeps the assets and liabilities of the company totally separate from your personal assets. It makes it possible to sale the business in stages by the selling stock in increments as you go.

If you plan to just support a lifestyle, then, at the appropriate time retire, a sole proprietorship may be the way to go.

If you are going into business with others and/or going to have to secure financing, an LLC or corporation should be looked at for the liability protection.

Are there certain employee benefits that you will need?

Take all of these factors into account to make your decision.

If after reviewing all of the items previously mentioned and you are still undecided, you might need to consult with an accountant or an attorney to help in the decision making process.

There are no laws prohibiting the changing of the form you choose later on down the road. There may be more complicated paperwork involved if you go from a corporation or LLC to a sole proprietor than from a sole proprietor to a corporation, but, it can be done. A lot of businesses start out as a sole proprietor and then as they grow and situations change; take a more formal structure for liability or tax reasons.

Again, the type of business entity you choose will depend on:

Liability - vulnerability

Taxation

Exit strategy

Nature of business

Figure 4-1 Items to Include in Partnership Agreement

When going into business with one or more other people you need to have a written agreement that includes the following:

1. Name, purpose, and location of business.

2. Duration of agreement or procedure for ending the partnership.

3. Names of all people involved.

4. Any financial contributions by partners, at inception or at any later date.

5. Role of each individual partner.

6. Authority of each partner.

7. Nature and degree of each partner's contribution to the business operation.

8. How business expenses will be handled.

9. How debt will be handled.

10. Authorization for signing of checks.

11. Division of profits and losses.

12. Method of accounting and recordkeeping.

13. Draws and salaries.

14. Absences and disability.

15. Death of a partner.

16. Rights of the continuing partner(s).

17. Employee management.

18. Sale of a partner's interest.

19. Settlement of disputes; arbitration.

20. Addition , alterations, or modifications to partnership agreement.

21. Non-compete in the event of departure.

CHAPTER 5
FEDERAL REQUIREMENTS

Do you need a Federal Identification Number (FEIN)? The answer is Yes. All of the forms of businesses, except sole proprietors, are considered separate entities and have to have their own identifying number. A sole proprietor may also consider a FEIN for two reasons. One—a number of your customers and/or vendors may require you to fill out a W-9 form. This form requires a tax number. You do not want to use your social security number. It is like giving you social security number to a complete and total stranger. Also, if you have employees, you would not want your social security number appearing on their W-2 forms. They could share it with anyone.

You can obtain a Federal Identification Number online at the IRS website or by filling out an SS-4 form and mailing or faxing it to the IRS.

Instructions for SS-4

Line 1: Enter the legal name *exactly* like you did with the state when forming your LLC or Corporation. Be sure to include every period and dash. If you are establishing as a sole proprietor, then enter your legal name as it appears on your tax returns.

Line 2: If you are a sole proprietor establishing under a fictitious name, enter the fictitious name here. If you are establishing as a corporation or an LLC do not put your name in Line 1 and company in Line 2. You put the company name on line 1 and leave line 2 blank.

Line 3: This is for trust, estates, etc. Leave this blank

Line 4: a-b Enter the mailing address for your business here.

Line 5: a-b Enter the physical address of your business here.

Line 6: Enter the county and state where your principal business location is located. i.e. if your store is in Alamance County, but, your home office is in Orange County. Put Alamance County, NC.

Line 7: a) Name of responsible party. Enter the name of the primary person starting the business. Responsible party is the person who has a level of control of the funds, assets and management of the business. b) Enter this person's social security number.

Line 8: a) if you have formed an LLC check yes, eitherwise, check no. b) enter the number of members in the LLC. c) Check yes that the LLC was formed in the United States.

Line 9: a) Type of Entity – put a check in the box that describes the form you chose for your business. If you are a sole proprietor, enter your social security number. If you are a corporation enter either 1120 or 1120S depending on your plan to file taxes as a Sub S Corporation b) If you formed a corporation enter the state you formed it in. i.e. NC

Line 10: Reason for applying. This might sound a bit confusing, but, most of you will check "Started a new Business" then you must specify the type. Here you would put retail, wholesale, service, or whatever best describes your business.

Line 11: Date the business started. Use the same date you used with the Secretary of State in filing your structure papers. If you are a sole proprietor and didn't file with the SOS, use the date you started or plan to start your business.

Line 12: Closing month of accounting year. This is generally December.

Line 13: You will enter the number of employees you expect to have in the next 12 months according to category. If you anticipate you will add employees sometime, but, are just not sure when, then enter zero. If you enter a number here, and then don't have any employees, you will still be required to file a quarterly payroll report. But, if you enter zero, then do end up having employees, you can file your quarterly report then, with no penalty.

Line 14: Check this box if you expect to pay less than $4,000 in wages. Your tax liability then should be less than $1,000 a year and you can file an annual report instead of quarterly reports.

Line 15: Enter the date you first expect to pay wages. If you are a sole proprietor and don't expect to pay wages, then you can enter NA for not applicable. Again, push this date out as for as you reasonably can so that if things don't go as planned, you aren't expected to file quarterly reports when you have no employees.

Line 16: Check the box that best describes the principal activity of your business.

Line 17: Write the principal line of merchandise sold, products produced, or services provided. This can be generalized for example: women's apparel, residential plumbing, etc.

Line 18: Check yes or no if you have ever applied for a federal id number under the name you listed in line 1. If you have a FEIN for the same name put that number in here.

Third Party Designee: Fill this portion out only if you want someone other than yourself to receive the FEIN and to be able to answer questions about the form.

After completing this form, we will now go online to request a FEIN. This normally takes about 5 minutes.

Go to www.irs.gov.

- Under "Tools" in the center of your screen – you will see.
- "Apply for an Employer Identification Number (FEIN) online". Click here.
- Scroll to the bottom of the page. Click on "Apply Online Now".
- Once you start the process you must complete it in one sitting. You cannot save the information and then come back later to finish.
- Be sure you have Adobe Reader installed on your computer.
- You will be taken to a screen with information pertaining to FEIN.   When you are ready, click on "Begin Application".
- You will then be taken to various screens for imputing the information from your S-4 form.

When you are through you will wait a few minutes and usually your new number will appear. Be sure to print the confirmation letter and keep it in your permanent records. I have known banks to ask to see the official paper and not just take a person's word for it.

If you do not have a computer or are uncomfortable applying online you can mail the completed form to:

Internal Revenue Service
Attn: EIN Operation
Cincinnati, OH 45999

Or fax it to: 859-669-5760

Most new businesses are unlikely to require any other federal permit or license to operate unless they engage in:

Rendering investment advice

Prepare meat products

Sell or produce alcohol, tobacco or firearms

Federal permits and licenses are also necessary to start some large scale operations in regulated industries such as:

radio and television stations

common carriers

or if you produce drugs or biological products.

Here is a brief listing of other business activities that require further licensing or registration:

Agriculture

If you import or transport animals, animal products, biologics, biotechnology or plants across state lines, you'll need to apply for a permit from the U.S. Department of Agriculture (USDA).

Aviation

If your business involves the operation of aircraft; the transportation of goods or people via air; or aircraft maintenance you'll need to apply for one or more of the following licenses and certificates from the Federal Aviation Administration:

FAA Licenses and Certificates - Get licensing information for airmen, aircraft, airports, airlines and medical aviation services.

Pilot Licenses and Training Requirements

Aircraft Mechanic Licenses

Fish and Wildlife

If your business is engaged in any wildlife related activity, including the import/export of wildlife and derivative products, you must obtain an appropriate permit from the U.S. Fish and Wildlife Service.

Commercial Fisheries

Commercial fishing businesses are required to obtain a license for fishing activities from the NOAA Fisheries Service.

Maritime Transportation

If you provide ocean transportation or facilitate the shipment of cargo by sea, you'll need to apply for a license from the Federal Maritime Commission.

Mining and Drilling

Businesses involved in the drilling for natural gas, oil or other mineral resources on federal lands may be required to obtain a drilling permit from the Bureau of Ocean Energy Management, Regulation and Enforcement (formerly the Minerals Management Service).

Nuclear Energy

Producers of commercial nuclear energy and fuel cycle facilities as well as businesses involved in the distribution and disposal of nuclear materials must apply for a license from the U.S. Nuclear Regulatory Commission.

CHAPTER 6
STATE AND LOCAL REQUIREMENTS

As stated earlier, every state and every county has a different process to go through in starting a new business. Generally, establishing an LLC or Corporation is handled through the state's Secretary of State's office. Establishing a sole proprietorship or partnership using a fictitious name is generally handled through the local county register of deeds office.

If you have employees or need to collect sales tax you will also need to register with your state's department of revenue. Things like unemployment, workers' compensation, minimum wage and other labor related issues are also handled by the individual states.

Figure 6-1 is a listing of state websites to get you started on satisfying the requirements in your state.

As of this printing, if you have a physical location in another state, you must collect sales tax for that state.

Some states consider a billboard as a physical location. Be sure to check in the states you do business in to make sure you comply with the sales tax laws.

There are states lobbying the US Congress to make it mandatory to collect sales tax in any state you do business, rather you have a physical location or not. Keep an eye out for this development. It will be a logistic nightmare for small businesses if it goes through.

Figure 6-1

Alabama	http://revenue.alabama.gov/licenses/index.cfm
Alaska	https://www.commerce.alaska.gov
Arizona	https://www.azdor.gov/Business/LicensingGuide.aspx
Arkansas	http://www.arkansas.gov/services/list/category/business-professional-licensing
California	http://www.calgold.ca.gov/
Colorado	https://www.colorado.gov/
Connecticut	http://www.ct-clic.com/Content/Smart_Start_for_Business.asp
Delaware	https://onestop.delaware.gov/osbrlpublic/Home.jsp
District of Columbia	http://dc.gov/page/permits-licenses-and-certifications
Florida	http://www.myflorida.com/taxonomy/business/business%20licenses,%20permits%20and%20regulation/
Georgia	http://sos.ga.gov/index.php/licensing
Hawaii	http://invest.hawaii.gov/business/permitting/
Idaho	http://www.state.id.us/business/licensing.html
Illinois	https://www.illinois.gov/Business/Pages/registration.aspx
Indiana	http://www.in.gov/core/business_guide.html
Iowa	http://www.iowaeconomicdevelopment.com/
Kansas	http://www.networkkansas.com/entrepreneurs/registering-a-business
Kentucky	http://onestop.ky.gov/Pages/default.aspx
Louisiana	https://geauxbiz.sos.la.gov/
Maine	http://www.maine.gov/portal/business/licensing.html
Maryland	https://egov.maryland.gov/businessexpress
Massachusetts	http://www.mass.gov/dor/businesses/help-and-resources/licensing-and-regulation.html
Michigan	http://www.michigan.gov/business
Minnesota	http://mn.gov/elicense/
Mississippi	https://www.mssbdc.org/resources/faqs#blicense
Missouri	http://business.mo.gov/register/index.html
Montana	http://revenue.mt.gov/licenses

Nebraska	http://www.sos.ne.gov/dyindex.html
Nevada	http://www.nvsos.gov/sos
New Hampshire	http://www.nh.gov/business/doingbusiness.html
New Jersey	http://www.nj.gov/njbusiness/licenses/
New Mexico	https://www.businesslicenses.com/Licenses/NM/
New York	https://bw.licensecenter.ny.gov/BW/guestHomeAction.els
North Carolina	https://edpnc.com/start-or-grow-a-business/start-a-business/
North Dakota	http://www.nd.gov/businessreg/license/index.html
Ohio	http://business.ohio.gov/licensing/
Oklahoma	https://www.businesslicenses.com/Licenses/OK/
Oregon	https://apps.oregon.gov/SOS/LicenseDirectory/
Pennsylvania	http://www.businessnation.com/services/licenses-permits/pennsylvania-business-licenses/
Rhode Island	http://www.ri.gov/business/index.php?subcategory=17&linkgroup=75
South Carolina	http://sc.gov/Business/Pages/licensePermitsAndRegistration.aspx
South Dakota	http://www.sdreadytowork.com/Build-Your-Business/Start-Your-Business.aspx
Tennessee	https://www.tn.gov/revenue/article/business-tax-registration-and-licensing
Texas	https://www.texas.gov/
Utah	http://www.dopl.utah.gov/renewal.html
Vermont	http://www.vermont.gov/portal/business/
Virginia	http://www.bos.virginia.gov/starting.shtml
Washington	http://www.dol.wa.gov/business/
West Virginia	http://www.business4wv.com/b4wvpublic/default.aspx?pagename=applyforlicense#resultsBookmark
Wisconsin	http://dsps.wi.gov/Licenses-Permits/Credentialing
Wyoming	http://ai.wyo.gov/economic-analysis/professional-licensing-board

CHAPTER 7
POLICIES AND PROCEDURES

By developing some policies and procedures when you first start out can help to keep you and your employees organized in times of crisis or chaos. Having systems helps to create a sense of safety. You and your employees will know exactly what needs to be done in any situation. Of course, some procedures and policies will have to be created and/or changed over time. But, having a few simple systems in place when you first start out can help eliminate headaches down the road.

A system is a process you follow. It's repeatable and makes it easier for someone else to step in and take over tasks for you. Having systems in place gives you and your employees an organized, simplified structure in which to work. A systemized business will free you, the business owner, to have more time to devote to strategy, innovation, and creativity.

We start by dividing your business into five areas of focus. These different areas have a lot in common even though they are totally different. These areas will sometimes overlap each other and even sound redundant, but, in the end, they all come together to make your business run as smoothly as possible.

- Customers – the backbone of your business

- Employees – the face of your business

- Vendors – work as partners in your business

- Finances – the decision making tools

- Taxes/Regulations – the unavoidable

By paying attention to these five areas, you put yourself into position to grow your business and reach your dreams. By evaluating each of the areas as you go through this section of the book you can then develop the tools to make sound management decisions. You will have the time and energy to focus on the really important aspects of running your business.

To be a successful and responsible organization you must have the ability to identify, locate, and retrieve the records and information required to support your ongoing business activities. Having the right information available at the right time depends upon your ability to quickly search through enormous volumes of data. Pinpointing complete and accurate information depends on having an efficient and intuitive set of procedures and tools.

Getting and keeping your business areas in top working order has numerous advantages.

- Makes it easier to make management decisions.

- Puts you in a better position if you decide to sell your business or to go public.

- Makes it easier for employees or family to step in if needed.

As you read this section of the book I'm sure you'll feel a bit over whelmed. It sounds like a lot of work and a lot of time- that's pushed to the limit as it is. I can assure you that a little time and work now will save you a ton in the future. Set aside a few minutes a day and before you know it your business will be organized and running smoothly. You will have the ability to take on more of the tasks needed to grow your business.

CHAPTER 8
CUSTOMERS

One of the most common reasons of business failure is losing focus on the customer. Let's face it, without customers you have no business. All the real value of your business is in your customers. Everything about your business has to be focused on providing products or services that draw customers to you, satisfies them, and brings them back. It makes sense to put the strongest emphasis on gathering, storing and using information about your customers. This information will help you to determine your target customer and better focus your marketing efforts. Having customer information makes it possible for you to focus your efforts on your customers' wants and needs.

Every business needs to record information about their customers. This information can be used in a variety of ways. From a financial stand point, you would use the information for reporting sales tax, knowing how much individuals owe you, and classifying your biggest customers. From a marketing stand point your customer information is vital to your marketing program and goals. You use your customer information to gain more customers and to target your products or services to the customers you want.

Targeting and Acquiring Customers

We begin by looking at customer information from a marketing stand point. The simple act of gathering customer information, in a convenient format, can give you numerous marketing opportunities. Having an updated, detailed record of customer data is critical for retaining and growing your customer base.

I find that an Excel spreadsheet can be one of the most beneficial methods of gathering data. A spreadsheet, when set up properly, can be used as a data base and the information 'merged' with a Microsoft word document, such as sales letters, envelopes, labels, emails, etc.

If you are using one of the popular accounting softwares, such as QuickBooks or Sage, you can keep an abundance of information about your customers right in the accounting software. This information can then be downloaded into Excel and used as a database.

If you prefer a manual method, index cards or a Rolodex are good choices. The most important thing is that you gather and use the information, how you store it is secondary.

The most basic information you need about every customer is: name, address, telephone number, and email address. Below is an example of an Excel worksheet set-up.

Last Name	First Name	Street	City	State	Zip	Telephone	Email

If needed, columns can be added for company name, birthdays, and other items unique to your business. By setting up this way (with separate columns for names and the address) you can better sort by name, zip code, etc if you want to send a promotion to a certain group of people. You can also see where your customers live, which can help you determine other vital marketing information such as, age, financial status, and marital status.

This marketing information is used to determine who your ideal customer is. This determines your target market. You use this information to design your marketing materials and methods of delivering this material. For example: if you find a large number of your customers are located in an area that is predominantly an older neighborhood made up of older baby boomers, email marketing might not work as well as mailers sent by US mail.

There are a variety of reasons businesses fail to acquire new customers. A few of the biggest reasons include:

– Your product or services are not as good as you thought they were. This is the time to really listen to your customers and figure out what would make it better.

– You're going after the wrong target market or you don't even have a target market. A lot of small business owners try to be all things to all people, causing them to waste both time and money going after the wrong markets. Again, listen to your customers. Keep details about your customers who do use your product/service to better narrow down your market.

– Bad spending or marketing decisions. This usually happens along with number 2. Knowing everything you can about your market enables you to direct your marketing directly to them. This also happens when you don't have a concise written marketing plan. One way to determine a good marketing approach is to see yourself as a consumer and how you respond to different marketing efforts. Note things that persuade you to make a purchase and see if the same methods will work in your business. As you gather information about your customers, determine the best way to reach them and the best way for you to accomplish this.

Retaining Your Customers

The above information is primarily used for marketing and acquiring new customers. To be successful in your small business you need to spend as much time keeping customers as you do acquiring new ones. This is done through customer service. Exceptional customer service means different things to different people in different businesses.

One of the main components of great customer service is consistency. You can achieve this by having detailed, written customer policies and procedures. Be sure to include how the following situations will be handled.

- Credit policies – Will you extent credit to your customers? What is the procedure for setting up an account? What are your credit terms? How will you handle past due accounts?

- Return policies – Will you accept returns? Is there a time limit for returns? Does the customer have to have the original receipt?

- Refund policies – Will you issue refunds or store credit? What documentation do you need for a refund?

- Conflict resolution – How do you handle unsatisfied customers and customer complaints?

- Discount policies – Will you offer discounts? What is the criteria for a discount?

By having this information clearly written out, you not only establish consistency in your customer service, but, you make it possible for employees to know exactly what is expected.

As you establish policies and procedures for handling customer service, be sure to set up procedures for recording and tracking sales. Follow the path from the first telephone call or visit to after sales follow-up. Have a clearly written procedure for how each step along the way will be handled. You can even have checklists and forms to make sure nothing is forgotten. Follow an order from the first contact with the customer until the money is put in the bank. Develop the easiest, but, most effective way to:

1. Write up/take the order

2. Fulfill the order

3. Ship the order

4. Invoice the order

5. Receive/process the payment

6. Follow up if payment is not received on time

Develop how you want each of these steps to progress into the next step. Be sure to write it all down.

You can use the same method and follow your other areas of the sales cycle, i.e. ordering product, receiving product, tracking inventory, etc.

Review your state's requirements for recording and paying sales taxes. You can use this as a guide for establishing your recording procedures.

In gathering information about your customers, you are responsible for maintaining the privacy and security of the information. Develop policies and procedures to protect this information.

CHAPTER 9
EMPLOYEES

Policies, procedures and job descriptions should be written out prior to hiring your first employee.

Job Descriptions

The first step to finding the right employee is to know what you need. Writing a job description will help you determine exactly what skills, experience, and behavior you want in your new employee. To write a job description, list the tasks that you want a particular position to be responsible for. For example, if you are thinking of hiring an administrative assistant, list the tasks you are performing throughout your work day and decide which ones you can have your assistant perform. This can also help you determine if it is really an administrative assistant or a bookkeeper or a customer service representative that you really need. You might also find tasks that could actually be eliminated.

Another approach is to list the areas that you have in your business in an "organizational chart" format.

Owner						
Marketing	Sales	Operations	Customer Service	Administration	Finance	Human Resources

Chart 9-1

As you go throughout your day, list the different tasks you perform under each classification. Make notes of areas or tasks that you are weak in. Chart 9-2 shows some of the various tasks/jobs that a normal business has to have to operate efficiently. This will not only help you develop your job descriptions, but also, aid you in deciding which positions you need to delegate.

The job description is also beneficial in targeting, training and determining compensation for your employees. Under certain labor laws there are situations (i.e. on the job injuries), where you need to know what an employee's "normal" duties are. By having written job descriptions, you not only protect your company, but, give guidance to employees.

Administrator	Accounts Payable Clerk	Accounts Receivable Clerk
Accountant	Budget Planner	Debt Collector
Expert	Educator	Finance manager
Fixer	Gofer	Goal Setter
Human Resource Manager	Insurance Planner	Invoice Clerk
Janitor	Job Coster	Marketing Strategist
Mail Clerk	Media Relations Manager	Networker
Payroll Clerk	Personnel Manager	Problem Solver
Purchasing Agent	Quality Control	Receptionist
Receiver	Shipper	Secretary
Technician	Trainer	Warehouse Manager

Chart 9-2 Business Tasks and Jobs

Having other people (employees) taking over the tasks that you don't like or don't know how to do can be the saving grace for many small business owners. By taking some of the burdens off of you, you can spend your time growing and cultivating your business.

Employee Handbook

Unfortunately, employees can throw employers an array of curveballs. You may be faced with absenteeism, tardiness, illness, family emergencies, maternal leave, false references, theft, weak excuses, irresponsibility, lying, quitting, alcohol or drug abuse, poor performance and poor customer service. Planning for these situations is critical for your business survival and your sanity.

Employees, like customers, strive on consistency. By having an effective employee handbook in place where you address how certain situations will be handled, you can not only comfort your employees, but, also protect yourself in legal matters.

One purpose of an employee handbook is to orient new employees with the company. It is a resource that provides answers for the most frequently asked employee questions. Besides informing new employees about company policy, a good handbook emphasizes the at-will nature of the employment and the company's disciplinary and termination rights. Most importantly, it is a declaration of the employer's rights and expectations.

An employee handbook should at a minimum cover the following:

- Attendance and punctuality policies

- Your pay period

- Breaks and lunch time policies

- Vacation and holiday policies

- Benefits and how an employee qualifies

- Safety policies – the procedure for handling a workplace injury; safety equipment to be used, etc.

- Inclement weather policies

- Policies against discrimination and harassment

- Any benefits legally required by your state. (i.e. Family Medical Leave)

- Policies and procedures for online and internet use. This is especially important if you use the internet to access accounts with your bank and vendors. Also, there are laws and regulations to follow if your customer's credit card and bank information is stored by your business. Make sure that you keep an updated listing of logins and passwords for employees. You don't want to be locked out of your accounts because an employee quit and you don't know the passwords.

At the beginning or end of your handbook, you should have a page where the employee signs that they have received the handbook. This page is then torn out and placed in their employee file.

Employee Files

You should have a file folder for each current employee, plus all past employees. In this folder you need to have their W-4's and I-9's, the page mentioned above from the employee handbook, their application or resume, emergency contact information, workers compensation claims, and any disciplinary notes. You can keep a record of their reviews and raises directly on the inside of the folder.

It is important to develop a policy that outlines the procedures for how your company will manage employee records and files. Be sure that your policies and procedures comply with federal and state regulations. Be sure to limit access to these files, by keeping them in a locked cabinet.

Establish a regular timeframe for reviewing and updating employment records. The IRS requires you to keep employment tax records for at least four years after the date that the payroll taxes were paid or due, whichever is later. Establish a secure procedure for disposing of employee records, such as shredding.

By having clear job descriptions, policies and operating procedures, you can rest easier when you are away from your business. You can better spend your time on tasks that benefit your overall company, and spend time growing your business.

Contractors

Some small businesses use people in their business they like to pay "under the table" or as contractors or casual labor to avoid paying payroll taxes. Word of advice – DON'T – unless they truly are contractors.

The IRS has very strict guidelines to distinguish between an employee and a contractor. Some states are even stricter than the IRS. Basically, if the contractor is not set-up as a business and does not file a Schedule C or equivalent tax return then they would be considered an employee. The fines, penalties, and back taxes could put you out of business.

If you do use legitimate contractors, be sure to get a W-9 completely filled out before you pay them for the first time. (More on this in Chapter 10). Set-up a file to house all their papers as you would a vendor.

CHAPTER 10
VENDORS

Without information and procedures for dealing with vendors, it would be hard to tell if they are taking care of you and your needs at the best price. By keeping certain information about your vendors you are in a better position to negotiate for better pricing and service. The first rule of purchasing is that "everything is negotiable".

Large companies have purchasing specialists. They are experts at researching the best quality for the best price. As a small business owner you can compensate for this by having information at your fingertips when you are researching and negotiating with suppliers. Many small business owners underestimate their own value as customers with their suppliers.

Other than the information you keep in your accounting software, the bulk of the information about your vendors can be best kept in a folder. Catalogs, paid invoices,

Certificates of Insurance, W-9's, can all be kept in one place, making it easier to find information when the need arrives.

A Certificate of Insurance comes from the vendor's insurance carrier and states which types of insurance they are covered under. A W-9 is an IRS form that states they are not subject to withholding taxes. It also provides their business structure and federal ID number.

Be careful when filling out paperwork that your vendors require of you. A lot of credit applications will require you to "personally guarantee" any charges your business incurs. Even if you are a corporation or LLC, you can be personally liable for charges your employees or partners make in the name of the business. Be specific on who can place orders and if you want a dollar limit on orders placed by anyone other than you or if you require purchase orders.

When filling out their paperwork, credit applications, or W-9's, do not supply your personal social security number. Use a federal id number, even if you are a sole proprietor.

Vendor management is an on-going process. You should hold periodic reviews and updates. Organizations are constantly changing. They acquire other businesses, introduce new products, move to new locations, and even go out of business.

A well-defined strategy and process for supplier selection and evaluation can help ensure quality and compliance. You will want to evaluate the financial health of your suppliers before signing contracts.

You may find it helpful, especially if you use accounting software, to design a simple "New Vendor Form" to aid you in gathering all the needed information. You would want to include:

Name

Address

Remit to address (Some vendors have a different address they want payments to go to.)

Telephone number

Fax number

Email address

Terms (When do they require you to pay your invoices? This information can come in handy when calculating cash flow projections. And, as a negotiating tool.)

W-9 On File

Federal ID number

1099 Vendor (Are you required to send the vendor a 1099?)

CHAPTER 11
FINANCES

Many small business owners shudder when they hear the words accounting or finance; but, it is one of those skills that the business owner needs even if you don't do the daily tasks involved. A successful business rests on sound financial recordkeeping. Without good records it is impossible to determine the financial condition or profitability of a business. By mastering some of the terminology and a few basic accounting skills, you will be better able to make sound management decisions as your business grows and prospers. (See business glossary in Appendix A).

Accounting has been defined as the language of business. The better you understand the language of business, the better you can manage your own business.

A key product of accounting is a set of reports called financial statements. Financial statements report business activity in monetary terms. The two basic accounting financial statements are the Balance Sheet and the Profit and Loss Statement. The balance sheet is a summary of your company's worth. It adds your assets and property together, subtracts the money that you owe other people and leaves you with the equity or value of your company. The profit and loss statement is basically what it says. It takes the total sales or income of your company, subtracts the expenses and leaves you with either your net profit or your net loss.

These financial reports are used in a number of ways. As stated above you use this information to make better management decisions. If you have outside investors they use financial statements to see if their investment was worthwhile. If you have creditors or people that you borrowed money or product from, they use the financial statements to make sure that you can pay them back. And finally, local, state and Federal governments use this information to levy income taxes, sales taxes and property taxes.

The first step in setting up your financial records system is to decide on the accounts that you want to use or in accounting terms the Chart of Accounts. The specific records and accounts a company needs depends on a number of factors, such as the type of business, the company's goals, your needs and interests, and cost factors. The system you use: manual, Sage, QuickBooks or some other computerized system, will defined the exact way the chart of accounts needs to be set up. Some computerized systems require that you use numbers while QuickBooks allows you to just use the words. The main thing right now is to decide how you want to track your financial information. A basic record keeping system should be simple to use, easy to understand, reliable, accurate, consistent, and designed to provide information on a timely basis. The chart below shows an example of a chart of accounts.

ASSETS		LIABILITIES	
100	Cash on Hand	201	Accounts Payable
110	Checking Account	210	Payroll Taxes Payable
115	Savings Account	220	Sales Tax Payable
120	Accounts Receivable	275	Loans Payable
130	Inventory		
150	Buildings and Land	EQUITY	
160	Automobiles		
170	Machinery and Equipment	300	Owner Contributions
175	Accumulated Depreciation	310	Owner Draws
		350	Retained Earnings
		375	Current Earnings
SALES/REVENUE		EXPENSES	
401	Product Sales	500	Cost of Goods Sold
405	Service Revenue	600	Advertising
450	Customer Discounts	610	Auto Expenses
475	Interest Income	620	Bank Charges
		630	Depreciation Expense
		640	Meals & Entertainment
		650	Miscellaneous Expenses
		660	Office Supplies
		670	Salaries and Wages
		675	Payroll Tax Expense
		680	Travel Expenses
		690	Utilities

Example of a Chart of Accounts

You can take this basic chart of accounts and customize it to fit your needs. For example, instead of just product sales you may want to know how much sales there are in a variety of products. You could break it down into Product A Sales, Product B Sales and so forth. Depending on your type of business, you may need to put more detail into your Cost of Goods Sold accounts.

Your accountant or bookkeeper can help you set up the exact chart of accounts that you need for your business and your tax returns. You are the only one who knows exactly what you need to track to make your business decisions and your chart of accounts may need to be a lot more detailed than what the IRS wants. See the following charts for how the IRS breaks things down on a typical business tax return.

Gross Receipts or Sales (Do not include things such as interest income or proceeds from the sale of an asset)

Returns and allowances (You do this separately because some states do not allow you to deduct discounts before you calculate sales tax)

Cost of Goods Sold (See next chart for how this is calculated)

Other Income (This is where you put interest)

Gross Income (Gross Profit + Other Income)

IRS Income Breakdown

Beginning Inventory

Purchases

Ending Inventory

Cost of Goods Sold = Beginning Inventory + Purchases – Ending Inventory

Cost of Labor – this is the direct labor associated with your product or service

Materials and supplies – this could include shipping supplies, screws, etc.

Other Costs – this could include shipping, etc.

IRS Cost of Goods Sold Calculations

Operating Expenses

Advertising	Pension and Profit Sharing Plans
Car and Truck Expenses	Rent or Lease
Commissions and Fees	Repairs and Maintenance
Contract Labor	Supplies
Depletion	Taxes and Licenses
Depreciation	Travel
Employee Benefit Programs	Deductible Meals & Entertainment
Insurance (Other than Health)	Utilities
Interest	Wages
Legal and Professional	Other Expenses
Office Expense	

IRS Expense Categories

One of the main reasons for breaking your expenses and sales into categories or accounts is to aid in making business management decisions.

The main concern of the internal revenue service is that you report every dime of revenue; and can accurately account for your expenses. We'll discuss this more in the next chapter.

By keeping your financial records current you not only make it easier to make management decisions, but also make it easier at year end to get your tax returns filed in a timely manner. It will also aid your accountant in making suggestions to help lower your tax burden. Be sure to set aside time to prepare and review your key financial reports.

You can set up a simple financial "scorecard" so you can easily spot trouble areas and areas where things are going as planned. Rate yourself on a scale of 1 to 10 (with 10 being totally satisfied) on how you feel your business is doing in the following areas:

Accounting & Reporting: How accurate is your accounting? How timely do you close out each month?

Accounts Receivable: How long does it take you to collect? Do you send out invoices in a timely manner?

Accounts Payable: Do you have a good payable approval process to protect against errors? Do you pay your bills on time?

Budgeting & Forecasting: Do you have a budget?

Cash Flow Management: How well do you manage your cash flow? Are you always scrabbling for cash?

You can use these ratings to see which areas need your attention.

Finance related issues can hamper the success of any startup. Some of the main problems include:

- Running out of cash
- Overemphasis on raising money instead of on customers or improving your product
- Sloppiness in keeping track of the numbers
- Failure to properly invoice customers
- Not following up on invoice collections
- Inconsistent pricing

And, the list goes on.

You can use the same method outlined in Chapter 8 and follow the other areas of your business, i.e. ordering product, receiving product, tracking inventory, etc.

One of the main financial tasks that you need to do before you open your doors is to create clear distinction between personal income/expenses and business income/expenses. This can best be achieved by opening a bank account and credit card for your business.

If you run everything through your personal accounts, you run the risk of losing tax deductions and you can't keep abreast of how your business is doing. If you are a

LLC or Corporation, you can potentially lose some of your protection against liabilities.

As your business grows, you may need to refine and perfect your procedures, but, the general ideas of how you want things done will already be implanted.

By having the issues resolved before you open your doors you increase your chances of survival tremendously. This is accomplished by having written procedures and guidelines in place.

CHAPTER 12
REGULATIONS/INSURANCE

The rules and regulations for record keeping for government agencies could fill the Empire State Building. Every state and local government has a different way they want things done. Most government agencies are primarily concerned with you reporting all of your revenue. One way to insure this is to be sure that you use invoice numbers on all of your billing. And, be sure to keep your invoice numbers in order and don't skip any numbers. Don't "delete" invoices. "Void" them instead and indicate why it was voided.

If you are a retail establishment using a cash register, be sure to "close out" your register on a regular basis, i.e. daily, weekly, etc. Just be consistent. Then make sure your deposits to the bank match your register reports.

In all but five states, businesses are required to collect sales tax. Each state is different as to what kinds of products or services are taxable. You can check with the department of revenue in your state to see what's taxable and what's not. You can then use this list as a guide to determine the categories or accounts you use to track revenue.

If you have a customer or customers who claim to be exempt from sales tax, be sure to have an exemption certificate on file. This would apply to organizations that are exempt from taxes (such as non-profits) and organizations that will resale your products. A sales tax exemption certificate is required to protect you in the event of an audit.

Probably the most paperwork and forms that you must keep on file have to do with employees. You must have a current W-4 on file for each employee. The W-4 gives you, as employer, permission to withhold federal income taxes from the employee's paycheck at the rate the employee specifies. If your state has income taxes, you must have your state's equivalent of a W-4 on file as well. The Department of Homeland Security requires that you have a completed Form I-9 on file. Form I-9 proves that a person is who they say they are and that they are allowed to work in this country. The form states that you have seen the employee's identifications. I would recommend actually photocopying their id's and keeping them on file as well.

You should keep receipts for all expenses you are claiming on your tax returns. The charts in Chapter 11 show the typical expenses a business has. You should also keep receipts and details about assets (machinery, equipment, etc.) that you purchase. This information is listed differently on your income tax returns as well as your city or county property tax listings. You also want to keep mileage records even if you drive a company car. I usually record the beginning mileage on January 1 in my day planner. This is the ending mileage for the previous year. The IRS requires that you enter the date, where you were driving to and why. It doesn't have to be elaborate, just enough to show it truly was a business related trip.

If you use a computerized accounting system, the IRS requires that you must be able to produce sufficient legible records to support and verify entries made on your returns. Your system must provide enough detail to identify the underlying source documents. Source documents are your original receipts, canceled checks, and credit card charge slips and/or account statements.

You must also keep a complete description of the computerized portion of your record keeping system. This documentation should detail the following items.

- What functions are being performed

- The procedures used to ensure that your information is accurate and reliable

- What controls are in place to prevent the someone from changing or deleting your records

- Chart of accounts and detailed account descriptions

A common question among business owners is "How long to I keep these records?" For most businesses, the answer is three years after the tax return was filed. There are of course some exceptions. If you did not report all of your income, you should keep you records for six years. If you filed a fraudulent return or did not file a return at all, you need to keep your records indefinitely.

You should keep records pertaining to assets for four tax years after you dispose of the property. For example, if you buy a piece of machinery in 2015, and sell the machinery in 2020, you will want to keep all the information (sales receipt from where you purchased it, repair invoices and paperwork from where you sold it) until 2025 (you will file the 2020 return in 2021, so four years later would be 2025).

All of the above time requirements are for the IRS. Your state or local government, insurance company, or creditors may have different requirements.

Insurance

Owning a business is risky. Even with proper research and planning you should expect the unexpected. Purchasing insurance moves most of the risk on to the insurance company.

Some business insurance is required by law in most states. Workers compensation, unemployment and disability insurances are required if you have employees. Rates, coverage, and requirements are handled by each individual state.

Some customers, depending on your industry, will require you to carry General Liability and other types of insurance, especially if you are working on their property.

CONCLUSION

Approximately 543,000 new businesses get started each month. In five years at least half of them will be closed. Some of the main reasons for this are:

- lack of planning

- lack of research

- lack of business operations knowledge.

This book has covered the key factors to consider before starting your own business. It seems like a lot, but, to ensure your success, the items and questions need to be thought out and answered.

I would love to have your input on the material covered in this book. Were there items left out? Was it too complicated? Too simple?

My aim is to help business owners succeed, your thoughts and suggestions are extremely welcome.

Please feel free to email me at:

startingout@catherinemmartin.com

I would love to hear from you!

Appendix A: Glossary of Common Business Terms

Accounts Receivable: This is money owed to you *from* other people.

Accounts Payable: This is money that you owe *to* other people.

Asset: This is something of value that you own, i.e. land, buildings, inventory, cash.

Balance Sheet: This is a financial report that shows everything you own, everything you owe and the equity you have in the business.

Breakeven: The point where revenue (sales) equals expenses. Or, how much you need to have in revenue to be able to cover all of your expenses.

CAPEX: This stands for capital expenditures. This is the expenses incurred to accumulate assets.

Cost of Sales (or COGS-Cost of Goods Sold): These are the actually cost or expenses that are directly related to your sales, i.e. cost of items you resale, labor to produce your products.

Depreciation: This is the loss of value of an asset over time.

EBIT: This stands for "earnings before interest and taxes". This is your net profit not including interest expense and income taxes paid.

EBITDA: This stands for "earnings before interest, taxes, depreciation and amortization".

Generally Accepted Accounting Principles (GAAP): These are the "rules" and practices that are considered the proper way to record financial information.

Gross Profit: This is your sales minus your cost of sales.

Liability: This items that you owe, i.e. accounts payable, taxes payable, loans payable.

Net Profit: This is your gross profit minus all your other expenses, i.e. rent, utilities, telephone.

P/L Statement: This is the Profit and Loss Statement. This represents your income and expenses for a given period of time.

ABOUT THE AUTHOR

Catherine M. Martin, a graduate of UNC-Greensboro's Bryan School of Business, has been helping small business owners succeed for over thirty years by offering accounting, management and training services. She is the author and creator of "Starting a Business in North Carolina" (2014) and "Taking Care of Business (2015). Catherine uses her expertise to educate small business owners in the management side of their businesses.

Catherine resides on a farm in rural North Carolina with her husband. She has three children and five grandchildren. Catherine spends her spare time writing, reading, sewing, crocheting and knitting.

If you have any questions about this book or its content, please email Catherine at startingout@catherinemmartin.com.

www.ingramcontent.com/pod-product-compliance
Lightning Source LLC
Chambersburg PA
CBHW070107210526
45170CB00013B/781